The Prestige
The Fifties

John Banks
Photography by David Burnicle

Cover: David Burnicle is a native of West Hartlepool and the local operator's Roe-bodied, centre-entrance unfrozen Leyland Titan TD7 No. **36** (**EF7380**) was a familiar sight to him during his formative years. Colour photography was not a practical proposition then, but an opportunity came in August 1984 when David was invited to Hartlepool (as it had then become) as a representative of Leyland for the undertaking's centenary celebrations. The Titan, by then long preserved by Bob Kell and in superb restored condition, was photographed in glorious colour, forming an appropriate link between the present and the past at the time.

Rear cover: The coaching scene in the 1950s was sharply defined: most large operators and some of the bigger independents bought heavyweight AECs, Bristols or Leylands, but the smaller independents often preferred lightweight Bedford or Ford chassis, usually bodied by Plaxton or Duple. **UDL453**, a petrol-engined Bedford SB3, actually registered in June 1960, fitted with Duple Super Vega coachwork and owned by the West Wight Bus Company, of Totland Bay, epitomised the "lightweight" sector. The decade also saw the last flowering of the trolleybus in Great Britain. Whereas many cities in mainland Europe and other parts of the world have continued to invest in the cleanliness and silence of electric traction, here in the UK the breed withered through the 1960s, became extinct in 1972, and city centres reel under massive amounts of exhaust pollution. The last system to survive was that at Bradford, whose No. **846** (**JWW376**), a 1950 Sunbeam F4, was originally a Mexborough & Swinton single-decker. It was rebodied as, relatively unusually for a trolleybus, a forward-entrance double-decker by Bradford in 1963.

Inside covers: Pages from David Burnicle's fascinating 1950s "time machine" album compilations.

Title page: "Shimmering salmon can" and "threshing machine" were two of the more printable epithets applied to Guy Arabs with Gardner five-cylinder engines and Metro-Cammell Orion lightweight bodies. They were hideous to drive and not very pleasant to ride in, but they were mechanically reliable and economical, considerations that far outweighed those of passenger, much less staff, comfort. Northern's No. **1654** (**CU7654**), with platform doors, was in Park Street, Middlesbrough, on the joint (with United) 55 service to Newcastle. The vehicle had been new in November 1955 and this is a circa 1957 photograph.

Opposite page: Southdown's 1939 Leyland Titan TD5 No. **218** (**FUF218**), was looking immaculate circa 1955, by then fitted with a 1949 Park Royal 54-seat body; it lasted until 1961. Within two years of this photograph Southdown's service 45 would be in the hands of new PD3 Titans.

Below: A nostalgic scene at Ringwood in 1955 with prewar and postwar Bristol Ls of the Hants & Dorset and Wilts & Dorset fleets. The anticipated Eastern Coach Works body on one of them contrasts with two less familiar by John C Beadle, of Dartford.

The 1956 Commercial Motor Show, bravely recorded from Earls Court's mezzanine with minimal equipment, with the Crossley and Leyland stands highlighted. The propinquity of Crossley's Bridgemaster and Leyland's Atlantean - both visible in these photographs - was perhaps the quintessence of the era's great sea-change, as buses with engines at the front that had to be worked by a crew of two began to give way to high capacity, front-entrance, rear-engined vehicles in which the driver controlled the doors and would eventually come to collect the fares as well. There were many reasons, some operational, some economic, some political, for the "rear-engined revolution" and 1956 can perhaps be seen as the "beginning of the end" or the "start of the beginning" according to the onlooker's viewpoint.

INTRODUCTION

This volume in the *Prestige Series* could well be subtitled "The Art of Low Tech Photography". All the pictures presented were taken in the 1950s on the most modest of equipment by a young enthusiast and they were all processed as contact prints from 3¼ins x 2¼ins or 2¼ins square negatives. "The *Art* of ..." because producing thus work of lasting merit was by no means easy and in those days many of us, one suspects, consigned our photographic efforts to the dustbin as too poor to keep.

David Burnicle was born and educated in West Hartlepool, Co. Durham. His father was a railwayman which meant that the young Burnicle was interested in railways from an early age. (This didn't always work: the writer's father had been a professional footballer and desperately wanted his son to be one, too. His efforts to force the game down said son's throat caused the latter to develop a lively and abiding hatred of the game. Now, had the parent been a busman ...)

David also had a leaning towards road passenger transport and he found it more accessible on his limited schoolboy budget. He then found that a schoolmate was interested in buses in particular, causing them to become friends and to pursue the hobby together. David tended to be interested in all the oily bits and his friend in all the rest. The circle has been completed because that friend was, and is, John Watson, also a native of West Hartlepool, who has given the writer valued assistance in the preparation of several of the titles in this series of books.

That phase of David's enthusiasm spanned the early 1950s until they each left town for different universities. The seeds had been planted for David to want to pursue a career in engineering and one involving vehicles and their engines.

David's first foray into taking pictures of buses was prompted by the imminent demise of trolleybuses in West Hartlepool, which led him to borrow the family Box Brownie and "take a few shots of them in poor light and in the wrong places but at least I got a record of sorts of a past era in the town". This ability of photography to capture and record for ever a specific point in time has appealed ever since and has led to the preparation of many albums of photographs, regrettably from one point of view not so many of buses in later years as they became a job rather than a hobby.

*Sources of bus photographs were legion. Bus stations were an obvious choice and at Scarborough on 6th June 1954 the photographer captured a typical mid-fifties mixture of prewar rebodied and postwar double-deckers and underfloor-engined single-deckers. East Yorkshire was the fleet and the vehicles were all Leylands: Nos. **557** (**LRH699**), **381** (**GAT67**) and **583** (**MKH92**). Coach parks, too, were always part of the itinerary: Keswick on 28th August 1953 produced a line of modern underfloor-engined coaches which were by then well on the way to relegating prewar and even early postwar front-engined coaches to the demotion cascade which saw many fine but allegedly uneconomic machines running as supremely comfortable stage-carriage vehicles. Standerwick's **121** (**EFV146**), a Duple Roadmaster-bodied Leyland Royal Tiger, was a solid, heavily engineered example of the new breed.*

The first 16 years of David's career were spent with Perkins Engines of Peterborough in various design, development and engineering applications posts. Not too many buses were involved at Perkins, except the odd Daimler Roadliner and Bristol LH, as the Perkins type of high-speed diesel was generally not accepted by the bus world which was still very much wedded to 1850 revs/min Gardner engines.

There then followed a most interesting period as the Technical Director of Leyland Bus Ltd when David was able to combine his early life interest in buses with the job of designing them. This was the period from 1977 to 1987. It started with finishing and launching the Titan, creating the National 2 (with a better windscreen and a proper busman's engine, the Leyland O680, and even a Gardner eventually), then on to the Tiger and the Olympian in two- and three-axle versions, the Royal Tiger, the Lynx, the L10 Tiger and others, and finished with the rail applications of the National body in classes 140, 141, 142, 155 and various railbuses in between. The rail projects were a means of trying to keep bus factories open in the face of the continuing growth of car ownership and the threat and eventual actuality of privatisation and deregulation of bus operation, which caused huge uncertainty in the bus industry at the time.

David then moved to be Engineering Director at Tickford Ltd: a world of so-called light-duty engines and vehicles (and, interestingly, the class 156 DMU and the BR Mark IV coach interiors for Metropolitan-Cammell). David semi-retired in 1998 and now works for Tickford part-time specialising in alternative fuel vehicles. This has involved the occasional bus (Optare NGVs for Cambridge and Reading) and various studies and prototypes of mini- and midi-buses, but not many "proper" buses, i.e. those with ten wheel nuts per wheel.

David's first phase of photography, which resulted in the set of albums from which the illustrations in this book are taken, covered the period 1953 to 1958 and was, as indicated above, achieved with modest means and equipment. David recalls that his meagre disposable income at that time (the writer, too, recalls being on 3s. 6d - 17½ pence - a week during that same period) did not allow any extravagance. There were eight shots to a film and every one had to count - no bracketing of exposures in those days!

The favourite operators were United Automobile Services and West Hartlepool Corporation. More pictures were taken of United than of any other operator. None, however, appears in this book. They are being reserved for use in the definitive, hardback, multi-volume history of United soon to appear from Venture Publications Limited. David's maternal grandparents lived on the Isle of Wight and many family holidays were spent there. This resulted in the Southern Vectis fleet becoming another major interest.

*Depot yards, provided one could gain entry, produced great riches. On 15th March 1953, Bee-Line's Foggy Furze, West Hartlepool, yard produced a fine variety of machinery typical of the larger independents of the day. Foden and Guy single-deckers (**GUP455** ex-Sutton, Kidsgrove; **CVN973** ex-Layfield, Thornaby) are visible and the double-deckers include **CUP261**, an ex-Stockton Corporation Daimler COG5 of 1938 fitted with Cravens bodywork. Bus garages were often harder to breach, but given a sympathetic foreman pictures such as this one, thought to be at Percy Main, Northumberland, in 1956 could be had. The single-deckers **W191** (**FT7791**) and **W176** (**FT7276**) were Beadle/AEC rebuilds in the Wakefields fleet.*

Between and around the two major areas of interest, however, lies a wonderful selection of pictures taken in most parts of the country, from Scotland to the south coast, from Hull across to Liverpool. When David made his collection available for this publication and the writer began to study the contents of the albums, it was like being in a time machine. More so than usual it has been hard to choose which pictures to leave out. On some pages smaller than usual images have been used (concomitant in some cases with the original prints being very small indeed and the negatives no longer being available) and it is hoped that the "amateur album" feel has to some extent been retained. This also means, of course, that there are more pictures than usual for a book in this series. It has been a fascinating technical challenge, too, working with these original contact prints and breathing new life into them for the enjoyment of readers almost a half-century after they were taken.

And what memories they evoke!

Saturday mornings, for example, spent wandering round the local bus garage, where the vehicles were all familiar friends. Perhaps an accident-damaged bus might be seen, or one on the ramp with all its wheels off. The foreman, surprisingly often a character sympathetic to young enthusiasm for the vehicles in his charge, if caught in amiable mood at a slack time, might well turn a blind eye as ticket boxes were scoured for mint additions to the collection (a handful of tickets once came out of a box nicely mixed with a half-eaten jam tart, but such were the hazards of the hobby). Members of the office staff - more relaxed on Saturday morning when senior management might not be present - could sometimes be prevailed upon to provide typed fleet lists and be prepared to scour store rooms for obsolete timetables, leaflets and tickets. Bus interiors might be explored and - the Holy Grail - cabs climbed into. The mere pressing of a button to open and close the doors on one of Hull's Coronation trolleybuses was fodder for excited boasting at school the following Monday.

Depot yards were slightly different. There was seldom an official specifically on duty in a depot yard, and such places were always full of buses (especially at the weekend) which exercised an irresistible attraction. Even when permission to take numbers and look for tickets was refused, as it occasionally and not unreasonably was, one had to walk through the yard to ask permission and then back out again and much could be achieved by dawdling.

Bus stations were splendid places and there was not the paranoia that sometimes obtains today about the presence of enthusiasts simply looking, drinking in the atmosphere, checking the routes and vehicles allocated to them, waxing lyrical about an unusual working (a single-decker on a double-deck route; a lowbridge bus from an outlying depot; a foreigner on a joint service) and even taking photographs.

Coach parks, particularly those at the seaside during outings and holidays, were to the small boy veritable Aladdin's caves. There might be the odd one or two private hire coaches from one's home town, but the riches to be seen from

*Fairgrounds and scrapyards harboured old friends pensioned off as well as vehicles too elderly to have been witnessed in passenger service. Doncaster Corporation's once-magnificent Roe-bodied Leyland Titanic **DT9642**, seen at Town Moor, Newcastle on 26th June 1954, was a shadow of its former self but still had great character and presence. This was typical of the lowered-roof conversions much favoured by showmen. Scrapyards were in some ways sadder places, for their inmates seldom escaped to run again, in however lowly a rôle. This was particularly so when vehicles known and loved in service a brief time before were witnessed in their dereliction. These 1938 ex-West Hartlepool trolleybuses - Nos. **1** (**EF6701**), **37** (**EF6897**) and **38** (**EF6898**) - were at Bainbridge's scrapyard, Thornaby on 10th October 1953.*

all parts of the country quite overwhelmed both mind and meagre photographic resources.

Then there were the scrapyards and fairgrounds which held an altogether different allure. Scrapyards in days gone by seemed to keep old vehicles for years. There was a prime example in Hull wherein several buses in the Corporation Transport Department's livery could be seen. These were buses which never ran as such in public service, consisting as they did of withdrawn bodies placed on withdrawn chassis (the good bodies from the time-expired chassis had been put onto newer chassis whose bodies - constructed using green timber - had proved beyond repair), the resulting combination being towed to the scrapyard. Some of those bodies still had tickets in the used-ticket boxes, or at least they did until discovered by Yours Truly.

Fairgrounds were another wonderland. Old buses by the hundred were once on a time employed by travelling showmen. Many were single-deckers, but double-deckers were almost as popular, usually with the upper-deck windows removed and the roof lowered. One which used to come to Hull Fair each October was an ex-Hull AEC Regent which still had a complete, legible blind behind the unbroken glass screen of the original destination box.

And then, of course, there were the streets along which the buses ran. Standing on the corner watching an unending stream of Corporation and Company buses, leavened with the occasional independent stage service or private hire working, was at least one youth's idea of bliss.

David Burnicle tapped all these sources of bus photographs with no little skill and organisation. This album attempts to use his work, on a tour of the country, to chart the bus and coach scene in the mid-1950s, of which little exists today, although David did photograph London Transport's prototype Routemasters whose very recognisable production successors are still running in the 21st Century.

At the head of these introductory notes is reproduced a pair of pictures taken at the 1956 Commercial Motor Show, midway through the decade and towards the end the photographer's period of activity. Nineteen-fifty-six was a watershed year for the bus industry, for at that Show were both a Crossley (in fact an AEC in all but name and badges) Bridgemaster and a prototype Leyland Atlantean, between them nicely illustrating the last gasp of the traditional bus and the first tottering steps of what has today become the huge 80- or 90-seat double-decker operated by a driver only. The Bridgemaster was only one of a number of low-height designs with the upper-deck seating laid out in the same way as in a highbridge design, and such vehicles helped the traditional, front-engined double-decker to stagger on for another dozen years or so. The type of design pioneered by the Atlantean, however, seems to be here to stay and who would be brave enough to foretell its demise?

What was outside Earls Court, on the streets, in 1956? Vehicles built in the 1920s could still be found, albeit it with showmen. From the 1930s there were whole fleets of buses - often rebodied - still giving yeoman service, whose value had been heavily written down but which were still earning revenue for their owners. The decade of the war and succeeding austerity years brought forth the utility body, built to a stern ministerial design which forbade curves and any form of individuality (despite which the various bodybuilders managed to clearly stamp their products with their identity). These utilities gave rise to the phenomenon, already touched on in the case of those supplied to Hull Corporation, of relatively new bus bodies becoming worn out through inadequacies in the materials used to build them whilst the chassis were good for many more years of service. The solution was to rebody or at the very least substantially rebuild and repanel them. Both sorts, plus a few originals, were about in their hundreds in the 1950s.

New chassis since the end of the war came from AEC, Leyland, Daimler, Crossley, Guy, Bristol and a host of smaller makers, Foden, Sentinel, Atkinson, Albion and Dennis among them. The list of body builders was a lengthy one. Such was the demand that almost anybody with a high enough door to their premises and an assortment of carpenters and panel beaters on the payroll could, and did, obtain orders to body buses and coaches. The great names - Weymann, Park Royal, East Lancashire, Northern Coachbuilders, Massey Brothers, Eastern Coach Works, Roe and so on - could afford to ignore competition from the smaller fry: their order books were full to bursting point; times were good and the living was easy.

Thus the prewar and wartime vehicles ran cheek-by-jowl with a splendid array of new vehicles from that encyclopaedia of greater or lesser manufacturers which totalled a vehicle-building industry able to cope, if at times only just, with all the country's requirements for buses and coaches. Where are they now? An operator can still buy a British chassis with a British body, but it has to be said that the choice is not vast.

The 1950s still had tramcars, too. Some systems had been under threat of closure, or even wholly or partially closed, during the preceding two decades when David Burnicle was photographing trams in Sheffield and Blackpool. Trolleybuses might have been thought to have had a brighter future. Not a few postwar orders from municipalities were gained, which in fact meant that when the systems were abandoned many scarcely worn vehicles were wantonly scrapped for lack of a new home.

The variety, then, which the photographer attempted to record for his own pleasure, of public road passenger transport, tracked or trackless, driven by electricity or the internal combustion engine, was immense. It is hoped that this selection from David Burnicle's collection will adequately portray that variety.

As always in these books, the notes and captions have been prepared with the help of a number of other enthusiasts. I am especially grateful to Philip Battersby and Ron Maybray, whose ability to identify a bus, and provide details of its history, from a mere registration number (and sometimes without it), has meant that the captions to David Burnicle's pictures are more detailed than they might have been; and to John Watson, who was standing alongside the photographer when many of the photographs were taken. His additional information and reminiscences have further enhanced the text. David and Mary Shaw have again acted as proofreaders and the eternal debt to the publications of the PSV Circle and The Omnibus Society is once more acknowledged with gratitude.

John Banks
Romiley, Cheshire, May 2001

Leeds 28th March 1954

WHITE HORSE RESTAURANT

SPORTS

Bournemouth 1955

FODEN - The remarkable diversity of smaller manufacturers (in this case only so far as chassis for passenger vehicles were concerned) whose vehicles ran alongside the greater numbers of AECs, Leylands, Guys and Bristols in the fifties cannot be better illustrated than with the products of the Sandbach, Cheshire, manufacturer Foden. Respectable quantities of double-deckers ran for certain municipalities, most notably and appropriately Chester and Warrington. Among the single-deckers to be seen was **AJC91** *(above)*, a PVSC6 model with Metalcraft 35-seat front-entrance bodywork. It was one of two, fitted with rear-axle sprag gear for use on the steep Great Orme route, new in May 1951 to Llandudno Urban District Council, which did not use fleet numbers. Both Llandudno Fodens were withdrawn in 1968. Ralph Bullock, of Cheadle, Cheshire, ran a Whitson-bodied Foden PVRG6, **PMB915**, seen *(below)* on private hire work at the seaside. The centre-entrance 41-seater had been new in 1953 to Hollinshead, of Scholar Green.

LONDON TRANSPORT PROTOTYPE ROUTEMASTERS - *Above:* **RM1** (**SLT56**) on route 260. The radiator grille configuration was an afterthought. When exhibited at the Commercial Motor Show in 1954, where it caused a considerable stir, RM1 had its radiator remotely mounted underneath the vehicle and had a much flatter (and more attractive) frontal treatment. When the radiator was mounted in the conventional position in front of the engine, the revised grille appeared. *Below:* London Transport inspectors were deep in conversation with the crew of **RM2** (**SLT57**) at the terminus of route 91. Although London's RT fleet had not had matching fleet and registration numbers, the Routemasters would have. The four prototypes (SLT56-59) did not, however, set the trend, although SLT56 did at least represent the year in which RM1 first ran in revenue-earning service. RM2 was originally green; it was repainted red for Central Area use in September 1957.

LONDON TRANSPORT STLs WITH NEW OWNERS

While the prototype Routemasters were causing no little interest and enthusiasm as the very latest thing in the Capital, many of London Transport's time-served buses of an earlier generation were provoking comparable interest in less glamorous fleets up and down the country. The independent Richardson Brothers, of West Hartlepool, collected a small fleet of former units of the STL class, including ex-STL925 (**CGJ62**) *(above)*, seen with another in Whitburn Street, West Hartlepool on 3rd August 1954. In the view below ex-STL1454 (**CXX207**) and ex-STL925 again, appear in a photograph at Richardson's yard in Spring Garden Road, West Hartlepool. The operator also had CLE37, DGX205 and EGO429, which were ex-STL1060, 1677 and 2358. All five ran until about 1958. In the background stands ex-West Hartlepool Guy Arab **EF7442** *(see page 24)*.

EX-LONDON TRANSPORT Q TYPE

These two shots of the former London Transport Q23 (**BXD544**) were taken in Bishop Auckland on 5th June 1954. The vehicle was running in the fleet of J J Baker Ltd, of Quarrington Hill, Co. Durham. Its livery was two shades of brown and cream. The proportion of ex-London Q-class vehicles to escape into subsequent ownership was perhaps smaller than with the STL and later utility and postwar classes; to see one was an occasion demanding front and rear views, despite the scarcity of film. This example had a Birmingham Railway Carriage and Wagon Company 35-seat body and had been purchased in 1953 by an operator named Robson, of Midgeholme, who ran it for a short time before it passed to Baker. It had a short life with the latter, being withdrawn in 1955 and used for spares. Also visible is ex-London Transport Duple-bodied Daimler CWA6 **GLX914** (ex-D42) in the fleet of Transport Motor Services (Bishop Auckland) Ltd.

EX-LONDON TRANSPORT UTILITY DAIMLERS

London's Daimlers, on the other hand, popped up all over the place and made as much of an impact, and for as long, in the provinces and abroad as they had done in the Capital. Ex-D8 (**GXE585**), a Duple-bodied CWA6 56-seater, was one of several acquired by Trimdon Motor Services in 1953. It is seen *(above)* in Park Road, West Hartlepool on 17th April 1954, shortly after being fitted with platform doors and repainted in the new TMS livery of blue and cream. It was withdrawn by TMS in December 1956. The Trimdon Motor Services fleet in April 1954 also contained ex-D60 (**GXV791**), another CWA6 56-seater, this time with Brush bodywork. When seen at Trimdon Grange *(below)* a week earlier - on the 10th April - it was still in London Transport livery with the TMS fleetname painted below the crudely obliterated London Transport transfer. This one lasted until May 1956. The Trimdon Grange premises were ex-Alton Brothers, acquired by TMS in 1952.

SENTINEL

Above: Trimdon Motor Services No. **9** (**PPT213**) was one of a trio, Nos 5, 9 and 7 (PPT212-214), of Sentinel SLC4s with Beadle 35-seat centre-entrance coach bodies, new in April 1954. Number 9 was in Oxford Road, West Hartlepool on 27th May 1954. It and No. 5 were later licensed to Bluebird, Middlesbrough, a TMS associated company. Number 9 was probably on hire to Richardson Brothers, whose garage was nearby.

Below: TMS Sentinel **OUP578**, seen on hire to Richardson Brothers at Wolviston Road, West Hartlepool, in 1954, was an STC6 with Sentinel's own bus bodywork to 44-seat configuration. The vehicle was a 1953 Sentinel demonstrator, originally registered JNT763. When sold to Trimdon Motor Services in February 1954 it was reregistered OUP578. It was withdrawn in 1960 and sold to Baddeley Brothers, of Holmfirth.

DURHAM INDEPENDENTS

Above: Trimdon Motor Services No. **18** (**CU3570**), a Daimler COG5, was ex-South Shields Corporation No. 114. It was originally fitted with 32-seat bodywork by Northern Coachbuilders. By the time of its sale to Trimdon Motor Services in 1952 it had gained the body from South Shields No. 106 (CU3204), a Weymann front-entrance 30-seater. It was photographed at Trimdon Grange on 30th May 1954 on the occasion of an Omnibus Society visit.

Below: Favourite Direct Leyland Titan TD5c No. **4** (**CUP253**), seen at Middlesbrough Exchange on 22nd April 1954, started life as Stockton Corporation No. 26 in January 1938. It then had a Cravens 52-seat body as on DPT344 *(see page 17)* but was rebodied as a Burlingham 56-seater in 1946; in the same year a conventional transmission was fitted. Favourite Direct acquired it in January 1951. In September 1955 the vehicle turned up in the fleet of Austin (Happy Days), of Woodseaves, Staffordshire, from which it was withdrawn in May 1958 and sold for scrap.

SUNDERLAND CORPORATION

Above: An evocative scene at Black Road parking ground, Monkwearmouth, on 1st March 1954 features Sunderland Corporation's Daimler COG5 No. **45** (**GR5216**) with radiator and bonnet well wrapped against the possibility of a late frost. A Roe-bodied 58-seater, No. 45 had been new in May 1938 and was sold for scrap not long after this picture was taken.

Below: Daimler **141** (**DBR41**), photographed in John Street, Sunderland, on 17th October 1953. This Roe-bodied 58-seater had been delivered the previous August as one of the batch with fleet numbers 140-147, which were the first vehicles delivered with route number boxes and the first to appear in Sunderland's new green and cream livery. Number 141 went to Berresford Motors Ltd, Cheddleton, in April 1967. It was not operated and was scrapped in 1968.

Ex-Stockton Corporation Daimler No. 72 (**DPT344**) in the Bee-Line fleet. This vehicle had been one of twelve COG5s with Cravens 52-seat bodies delivered to Stockton in 1938. Bee-Line acquired it in 1952 and ran it until the end of 1954. The picture was taken at Bee-Line's Oxford Road, West Hartlepool, garage.

A VISIT TO THE PLAXTON FACTORY

JUP646, a 1949 Commer Commando from the J Tulip & Son, Throckley, fleet, was the splendid conveyance for an Omnibus Society visit to Plaxton's Scarborough factory on 26th June 1955. The Commer's 30-seat coachwork was appropriately by Plaxton - a diplomatic touch. The vehicle had been new to T Curry, of Seaham, before passing to Tulip. The stacks of timber, then much used in composite coachwork construction, seen in the upper picture would have been weathering before use. The writer visited Plaxton's in April 1998: 43 years on, timber was conspicuous by its total absence in the very different integral all-metal construction by then in vogue.

A VISIT TO THE PLAXTON FACTORY

In these interior views a number of vehicles are seen in various stages of bodying: from, in fact, a completely bare AEC Reliance chassis *(above)* to a completed petrol-engined Bedford SBG with 36-seat coachwork *(below)*. The latter was **MNT540**, which is recorded as being new in July 1955 to Elcock, of Ironbridge. The vehicle alongside the Bedford is thought to be a Commer TS3. The composite building methods of a half-century ago can be seen. They contrast with today's all-welded technical masterpiece. There is indeed a wide gap between yesterday's craftsman, whose work was equally a masterpiece in its own right, and today's high-tech engineers. Each has an honoured place in the transport eras they respectively serve.

NORTHERN GENERAL SINGLE-DECKERS

These remarkable vehicles chose themselves for inclusion. Northern's **655** (**CN6614**) *(above)* was a Northern-built NGT SE6 chassis, originally with a Short Bros 28-seat coach body, which had been new in July 1935. It was rebuilt in 1937 by Duple, when extra ventilation grilles were fitted and the front grille modified. CN6614 was withdrawn in 1954 after 19 years of service. It still managed to find a purchaser in the shape of Yardley's Perfumes, London E15, presumably as staff transport, with whom it lasted until 1958. Number **667** (**CN6626**) *(below)* was a similar chassis, new in September 1935, which had a Short Bros 44-seat bus body from new. It was also withdrawn in 1954 and for 19 years was a regular sight on the Tyneside services. These photographs of coach and bus versions of essentially the same vehicle were taken at Keswick coach park on 23rd August 1953 and at Marlborough Crescent bus station, Newcastle on 1st July 1953.

NORTHERN GENERAL SINGLE-DECKERS

Above: A variation on a theme was the Northern-built NGT SE4 model sporting, as its designation suggests, four instead of six wheels. Number **822 (CPT922)** was new in January 1939 as a front-entrance 40-seater bodied by English Electric. It was photographed on 26th June 1954 near Worswick Street bus station, Newcastle. Numbers 821-826 were the last SE series vehicles built by Northern. It had by then proved possible to fit 38 seats into a conventional chassis and Northern had standardised on the AEC.

Below: The last of the batch 1543-1557, No. **1557 (DCN857)**, was a Saro-bodied 44-seat Leyland PSUC1/1 Tiger Cub of 1954. Further similar vehicles were bodied by Weymann. Northern's Tiger Cubs performed with gusto over the hilly terrain of West Durham. Despite the "Newcastle Worswick Street" destination blind, No. 1557 was at Marlborough Crescent bus station in this 1955 photograph.

WEST HARTLEPOOL CORPORATION

Above: WHCT No. **26** (**EF6726**), seen at West Hartlepool depot on 29th May 1954, was one of a pair of Daimler COG5s with Roe front-entrance 35-seat bodies delivered in April 1938. Both were acquired by Trimdon Motor Services in December 1955. The erstwhile No. 26 lasted but a short time with TMS, being withdrawn in 1956. It became a static caravan at Hart Station. *Below:* AEC Regent No. **34** (**EF7378**) at West Hartlepool depot yard on 29th May 1954. This was one of a pair with 7.7-litre engines and Roe 48-seat centre-entrance bodies on unfrozen chassis which were diverted from Sunderland Corporation *(as the body mouldings reveal: see Sunderland's GR5216 on page 16)* while at the bodybuilder. Unfrozen chassis were those which were in build when war broke out in 1939 and were stopped (or "frozen") by ministerial decree, which was later rescinded, allowing completion of the chassis - hence the description "unfrozen".

WEST HARTLEPOOL CORPORATION - *Above:* WHCT No. **36** (**EF7380**) on 11th May 1953. Our cover subject is seen in service in West Hartlepool long before its recruitment into the ranks of preserved buses. Number 36 was a Leyland Titan TD7 with Roe 48-seat centre-entrance bodywork which had been new in July 1942 on an unfrozen chassis. It was withdrawn in 1958 and in December 1962 was sold to Bob Kell, then of Stokesley, North Yorkshire, for preservation. It was in fine fettle 22 years later in 1984, as seen on the cover, and in 2001 is still owned by Mr Kell. *Below:* Centre-entrance Daimler No. **49** (**EF8283**) was one of eight CVG6s with Roe 50-seat centre-entrance bodies. These were the last centre-entrance and the first eight-feet-wide buses in the fleet. All subsequent orders would specify standard layout with rear entrances. The batch, including No. 49, were rebuilt by Roe as rear-entrance 59-seaters in 1959. Number 49 was withdrawn in 1962.

WEST HARTLEPOOL CORPORATION

Above: WHCT Guy Arab I utility No. **42** (**EF7442**) fitted with Pickering bodywork, photographed on 8th June 1953. New in November 1943 in the darkest days of the war, No. 42 was withdrawn in 1953. It went on to brief further service in its home town with the independent Richardson Bros, before passing to a fairground showman who carried out a roof-lowering conversion. EF7442 was last licensed in September 1960. Number **43** (**EF7443**) of the same type stands behind No. 42. *Below:* WHCT Daimler 56-seater No. **44** (**EF7483**) was the only Brush-bodied utility in the fleet. It dated from March 1945 and was withdrawn in 1958. The vehicle is not known to have run again after passing to the dealer North's, Leeds, in October 1958. This photograph was taken in happier times, on a murky and misty 28th April 1953.

WEST HARTLEPOOL CORPORATION

Above: WHCT Daimler No. **52** (**EF8286**), another of the last batch of centre-entrance Roe 50-seaters on CVG6 chassis, photographed on 10th June 1953. Following its rebuild in 1958 as a rear-entrance 59-seater, No. 52 was withdrawn in June 1964 and sold for scrap. *Below left:* WHCT **45** (**EF7529**) was a Daimler CWD6, one of three Massey-bodied rear-entrance 56-seaters dating from February 1946. It was photographed on 7th March 1953. *Below right:* WHCT Daimler No. **56** (**EF8558**) taken on 7th March 1953. Although not the operator's first rear-platform double-decker (the wartime utilities had introduced that configuration), this Roe-bodied CVG6, delivered in November 1948, was the vehicle, coming immediately after the 1948 centre-entrance Daimlers, which started the programme for all future vehicles to have rear platforms. Number 56 was exhibited at the 1948 Commercial Motor Show, hence the chromium-plated radiator shell.

HARTLEPOOL CORPORATION -- Neighbouring Hartlepool Borough Council, wishing to be independent, in 1953 placed in service a fleet of four ex-London Transport utility Bristol 56-seat double-deckers: three Duple-bodied and one Park Royal. They were first overhauled at Darlington Central Works by United Automobile Services Ltd, the intention having been that United would operate them on behalf of Hartlepool. Union troubles centred on differing rates of pay in the municipal and company sectors stopped that plan and the buses were operated and staffed by Bee-Line Roadways. No. **H1** (**HGC238**), ex-London fleet number B13, was one of the Duple-bodied AEC-engined K6As, seen *(above)* on 15th August 1953 in Church Street. The other K6As were HGC239 and 253, ex-London B14 and B28. All had been new to London Transport in 1945/46. The Park Royal-bodied unfrozen version of the London Transport Bristol, which dated from 1942, is represented *(below)* by No. **H4** (**FXT423**), ex-London B5 and originally a K5G, which was photographed on 2nd August 1953 - the second day of operation of the new Hartlepool "blue buses" - in Clarence Road outside United's West Hartlepool depot.

>> *Opposite page:* The ex-London Transport Bristol Ks were replaced in 1956 by a fleet of four handsome blue and cream AEC Regent Vs, represented by No. **3** (**TUP858**) in two May 1956 Church Street views. The 63-seat rear-entrance bodies were by Roe. All four passed to the amalgamated Hartlepool Corporation Transport in 1967, as fleet numbers 95-98, and were repainted from blue to red, when the two boroughs, Hartlepool BC and West Hartlepool CBC, were merged.

NORTH OF THE BORDER -- 1

The vehicles of certain operators in the fifties - London, Birmingham and Manchester spring to mind - were instantly recognisable as having a style and appearance all their own. Their orders were big enough for bodywork suppliers to cater to individual requirements. Glasgow was another such operator. The AEC Regent V, No. **A282 (FYS588)** *(above)*, was new in November 1955 and was one of a batch of Alexander-bodied 60-seaters (A266-340) which unusually had Gardner 6LW engines. Albion CX19 **B26 (EGA32)** *(below left)* had MCCW 56-seat bodywork and had been new in January 1949. It became a driver-training bus in October 1958 and was withdrawn in March 1962. Daimler CVG6 **D114 (FYS569)** was one of 49 Weymann-bodied 60-seaters delivered in 1955. It lasted until 1969 before being withdrawn and sold for scrap.

NORTH OF THE BORDER -- 2

Above: Dundee Corporation's association with Daimler began in 1931 and continued until 1975 and the formation of the Tayside Regional Council. Dundee's veteran No. **25** (**YJ5892**), a 1938 Daimler COG5 with English Electric 36-seat centre-entrance body, was withdrawn in 1958.

Right: When the London Transport Weymann-bodied postwar STLs were withdrawn in their prime, they were eagerly acquired by various operators, including Dundee. Ex-STL2685 was running as Dundee's No. **171** (**HGC218**).

Below: Dundee's tower-wagon No. **2** (**YJ4113**) was a conversion from a 1937 Daimler COG5 centre-entrance single-decker.

NORTH OF THE BORDER -- 3

Above left: Alexander Guy Arab **RO720** (**GYL449**), an ex-London Transport wartime utility.

Above right: Central SMT Leyland Titan **L334** (**CVD534**) of 1951 had Northern Counties lowbridge 53-seat bodywork.

Left: Lawson of Kirkintilloch utility Guy Arabs **RO678** (**CAV237**) and **RO455** (**AMS42**) had been transferred from the Alexander fleet in 1952 and 1945.

Below: A pair of Bristol Lodekkas in fine original condition in the Lawson fleet. **RD16** (**GWG992**) and **RD19** (**GWG995**) were 1956 LD6Gs with 60-seat Eastern Coach Works bodywork. The Lodekka was highly regarded by the Scottish major operators.

NORTH OF THE BORDER -- 4

Above: Leyland LT5B single-decker **FG9464** was fleet number **P191** in the Alexander fleet. It had been acquired in May 1937 from the General Motor Carrying Company Limited, of Kircaldy. The vehicle had been new in May 1934 and had been fitted with a Leyland 8.6-litre oil engine in 1935. The 32-seat front-entrance bodywork was by Alexander. It was withdrawn as a 22-year-old in 1956.

Below: Alexander's Guy Arab III single-decker **BMS860** was fleet number **G90**, one of 30 (G72-101) Gardner 5LW-engined machines with Guy 35-seat bodies, which had been new in 1948. G90 was sold in May 1961. Both the pictures on this page were taken at Leven, Fife.

CUMBERLAND TITANS

Above: Cumberland's 1952 Leyland Titan PD2/12 No. **332** (**LRM106**), seen on a wet and murky 28th August 1953 in Keswick, was one of a batch of ten (328-337) with 55-seat Leyland lowbridge bodies. In December 1961 this bus was renumbered 394 and it was withdrawn in 1970.

Below: The 1953 summer weather had been much better at Whitehaven depot a week earlier when ex-Southdown prewar Titan **UF8845**, running as Cumberland No. **99**, was photographed on 21st August. Number 945 in the Southdown fleet and new in June 1932, UF8845 came to Cumberland in September 1940, fitted with a Short Bros 50-seat body. It was rebodied with a Burlingham 54-seat unit in 1948 and withdrawn later in 1953, when its body was reused on Leyland Titan TD5 No. 143 (DRM7), which then lasted until 1959.

BLACKPOOL

Above left: Number **158** (**FV9000**), one of 75 Burlingham-bodied Leyland Titan TD4 and TD5 models put into service in 1936/7. All lasted into the mid-1950s. *Above right:* Number **298** (**EFV298**), a postwar 8ft-wide Titan PD2/5 (one of 100), again bodied by Burlingham, did a world tour in 1970. It was scrapped in 1979. *Right:* **BFR380** was No. **15**, one of six Burlingham-bodied Leyland Tiger TS8s new in July 1940. It lasted in service to 1960. *Below left:* One of trams Nos **10-21**, English Electric BT56Cs on English Electric bogies dating from 1939. *Below right:* Fleet numbers on Blackpool's prewar tram fleet were placed above the centre entrances, making identification difficult or, in most three-quarter views, impossible. This is one of the English Electric single deckers (Nos **200-224**, **264-283**) of 1934/5. All these pictures come from the same day, circa 1956.

LIVERPOOL

Above left: **A170 (FKB358)** was one of 30 AEC Regents bodied by Liverpool Corporation on Weymann frames. Liverpool did not use fleet numbers until 1947. *Above right:* **A192 (GKA275)** had an unfrozen AEC Regent chassis with Weymann bodywork. It was sold for scrap in October 1958. *Left:* One of 100 AEC Regent IIIs new in 1948/9, No. **A335 (HKF811)** was bodied by LCT on frames supplied by Weymann of Addlestone. *Below left:* **D545 (JKC170)** was one of a batch of 50 Daimlers. Most had AEC 7.7-litre engines, but D545 was one of ten fitted with the Daimler CD 8.6-litre unit and was thus a CVD6. The 56-seat body was by Northern Counties. *Below right:* **A780 (MKB973)** was one of 50 8ft-wide Crossley-bodied AEC Regent IIIs new in 1951/2. All 50 were scrapped after their Liverpool service, none surviving to run for second owners.

LIVERPOOL -- *Above left:* Weymann-bodied 1952 Leyland Titan PD2/12 **L844** (**MKB927**) at Seaforth in January 1957, in a minor collision with a Morris saloon car. The latter was registered in Oxford, perhaps owned by a visitor unused to Liverpool's streets. *Above right:* **A1** (**NKD501**) was an exhibit at the 1952 Commercial Motor Show. It was one of a batch of 100 AEC Regent IIIs, 98 of which were Crossley-bodied. The design of the front panelling was Liverpool's own. *Right:* Slightly different "tin-front" styling on Weymann-bodied Leyland Titan PD2/20 **L209** (**SKB206**). *Below left:* Liverpool tried unpainted buses for some time. This one is AEC Regent **A40** (**NKD540**), which was one of two (A39/40) in the batch A1-A100 to have SARO 58-seat bodies. *Below right:* **SL173** (**SKB170**), a 1956 Leyland Royal Tiger, newly in service on the 77 to Penny Lane via Dale Street. Its 40-seat dual-door body was by Crossley.

WALLASEY and BIRKENHEAD

Above: Wallasey Corporation No. **105** (**CHF564**), a 1955 Burlingham-bodied Leyland Titan PD2/10, photographed in September 1956. The body dated from 1949 and had been fitted to an earlier No. 105, registered HF5226, a 1936 Leyland Titan TD4c. *Below:* Birkenhead Corporation No. **127** (**ACM302**) seen in the same month. This Massey-bodied Leyland PD1 dated from 1948. Massey first provided bodywork for Birkenhead buses in 1931 and was to be the major supplier until 1967; during that period a total of 401 Massey bodies entered Birkenhead service.

CROSVILLE

Above: Leyland-Beadle **PC25** (**LFM241**), seen at Llandudno in September 1956, was one of 20 built in 1950 using the running units, radiators and 4.7-litre engines from 1937 Leyland Cubs. Most of these 35-seaters gave almost a decade of service. *Below:* **KW177** (**LFM758**) at Llandudno in September 1956. This 39-seat Eastern Coach Works-bodied Bristol LL6B was new in 1950 and withdrawn in 1967 as fleet number SLB177. Painted-out rear destination screens and a letter-box are distinguishing features. Although the letter-box must have made the bus more then 30ft long, it is believed that this was permitted because the extension was temporary and detachable, much in the way that an overhanging load on a lorry would temporarily increase its overall length: a situation specifically catered for and allowed under the Construction & Use Regulations.

SOUTH LANCS TROLLEYBUSES

South Lancs trolleybuses on 6th March 1957. Vehicles featured are No. **4 (TF2075)** *(right)*, a 1930 Roe-bodied Guy BTX 70-seater; No. **13 (TF5240)** *(above left and right)*, a similar vehicle, seating 66, dating from 1931; No **53 (BTE952)** *(below left)*, a Roe-bodied 64-seat Leyland TTB4 dating from March 1937, which had been slightly rebuilt with a plain front; and No. **71 (HTD868)** *(below right)*, a Weymann-bodied Sunbeam MS2 64-seater of 1948. All these trolleybuses survived until the closure of the system in August 1958. Numbers 4 and 13 were in origninal condition. Number 71 was decorated and ran as the last SLT trolleybus; on the day following the closure, it made a ceremonial return journey from Atherton depot to Leigh. As SLT had been dissolved the day before, No. 71 was operated by Lancashire United Transport Limited for one day.

SHEFFIELD

Above: An evocative scene inside Queens Road Works in April 1958. AEC Regent **245 (LWB745)**, a Cravens-bodied AEC Regent III of 1950, was in for attention. This body was very similar to those supplied to London Transport as part of the RT class. *Below left:* Daimler CWD6 No. **90 (HWB480)** was new in 1945 with Brush bodywork. It was rebodied by Roe as a 56-seater in 1953 and withdrawn and sold for scrap in June 1962. *Below right:* AEC Regent III No. **751 (WWB751)** was new in 1956 with Weymann bodywork. It survived to 1970.

SHEFFIELD and ROTHERHAM

Above left: Number **228** (**NWA928**), one of three 44-seat Weymann-bodied Leyland Olympics of 1951. *Above right:* Believed originally in the fleet of Branson, of Chesterfield, Leyland LT3 Lion **VO7445** came to Sheffield during the war from the Ministry of Supply. It had been converted for use as a canteen, was put into service as such on 23rd January 1943 and lasted until March 1958, when it was replaced by a Leyland PS1 similarly converted. *Right:* Sheffield Transport Department tramcar No. **456**, one of 50 built in 1927 by Cravens with MV102 motors. It served Sheffield for 30 years. *Below left:* Rotherham Corporation Daimler CTE6 trolleybus No. **84** (**FET344**), dating from 1949. The East Lancs body had 38 seats. *Below right:* Rotherham Daimler CVG6 No. **235** (**PET235**) with Weymann 59-seat bodywork; new in 1957, it was withdrawn and sold for scrap in August 1972.

DONCASTER

Above: Doncaster Corporation trolleybus No. **362** (**BDT127**), originally numbered 62, was a one of a batch of 20 Karrier E6s with Roe 60-seat bodies delivered in 1939. This vehicle went on loan to Rotherham Corporation in 1955 for a series of clearance tests, prior to the introduction of double-deck trolleybuses on that system.

Below: Trolleybus No. **385** (**BHJ828**) in the Doncaster fleet was a Sunbeam W with Park Royal 56-seat utility bodywork, which had been new to Southend Corporation as fleet number 131 in August 1945. It was sold to Doncaster in January 1954 and in December 1958 was rebodied by Roe as a 62-seater. Withdrawn in 1962, its Roe body was transferred to a diesel-engined bus, Daimler CVG6 No. 184 (584HDT).

HULL CORPORATION -- Above: AEC Regent III No. **338 (OKH338)**, one of six new in October 1953. These Weymann Aurora 58-seaters were the first 27ft-long by 8ft-wide buses in the Hull fleet. The writer rode on this bus during its first week in service and still considers it to represent one of the most attractive double-deckers ever built. Number 338 was withdrawn in 1971 and sold for scrap. Similar bus No. 337 was under preservation back in the 1970s. Does it still exist? **Below:** Hull's trolleybus fleet was one of the most distinctive in the country. In these two views at Queen Victoria Square on 2nd March 1957, 1938 Cravens-bodied Crossley TBD4s No. **29/45 (ERH29/45)** are contrasted with 1955 "Coronation" Sunbeam MF2B No. **114 (RKH114)**. There were 16 of these Roe-bodied dual-doorway 54-seaters (Nos 101-116). When the system closed on 31st October 1964, these vehicles were barely nine years old. In one of the greatest and most wasteful scandals of the whole sorry story of the rundown of the British trolleybus network, all 16 were scrapped at a time when there were other systems - albeit not very many - still running electric traction. Nos 29 and 45, on the other hand, lasted respectively into their 22nd and 23rd years. These pictures show out-of-service, terminal turning movements: with five of the six major routes on headways varying from two to twelve minutes terminating close by in Paragon Street and King Edward Street, this sort of trolleybus procession through Queen Victoria Square was constant throughout the day.

BIRMINGHAM

Above: All-Crossley DD42/7 No. **2410** (**JOJ410**) of 1950 and 1952's MCCW-bodied Guy Arab IV No. **2916** (**JOJ916**) on service 62 to Rednal. These Guys had Gardner 6LW engines and preselector gearboxes, bringing their specification up to that of the Daimler CVG6s in the fleet. The Crossley lasted 15 years but the Guy served 19, ending up with the West Midlands PTE. *Below left:* Daimler CVG6 No. **3227** (**MOF227**), a 1954 Crossley-bodied 54-seater, also lasted into WMPTE days and was not withdrawn until 1977. *Below right:* Among the most fascinating of early postwar double-deckers was the combination of the ultra modern AEC RT chassis and Park Royal's version of the somewhat conservative Birmingham style of bodywork. Number **1634** (**GOE634**), one of 15 new in 1947, was withdrawn in 1963.

WEST BROMWICH

Above: A radiator top-up from a handily placed watering can at a bus stop on service 74 for Daimler **96** (**AEA26**) on 2nd April 1957. This MCCW-bodied COG6 was one of 31 received in 1939 for tramway replacement. It was withdrawn as a 21-year-old and broken up by the Corporation in December 1961. *Below left:* Daimler **75** (**AEA5**), another of the same batch, on 2nd April 1957. *Below right:* In a traffic jam on its way to Wednesbury on 1st April 1957, 1940 Daimler COG6 **107** (**BEA37**) displays its rare Jensen 38-seat bodywork.

WALSALL

Clockwise from above: Crossley-bodied Bridgemaster No. **825** (**YDH225**) was at the 1956 Commercial Motor Show and the 1957 Scottish Motor Show; Park Royal-bodied Guy Arab **132** (**ODH90**) was new in 1951 and scrapped in 1968; Leyland Titan **812** (**RDH502**) was one of ten PD2/12s with bodies completed by Roe on Park Royal frames; trolleybus No. **302** (**FTG698**) was one of several second-hand trolleybuses acquired from various sources by Walsall. It was a 1946 Roe-bodied Karrier W which came from Pontypridd UDC in 1955. It ran until 1962 when it was sold for scrap; Perkins-engined Bedford SBO **298** (**XDH298**) was one of six with Willowbrook 39-seat bodies acquired in 1956. This vehicle was converted to a mobile staff canteen in April 1968 and passed to the West Midlands PTE, "serving" in that capacity until June 1973.

HANTS & DORSET

Above: Leyland Titan TD2 No. **967 (LJ7097)** was new in 1933, fitted with a Brush body. It was fitted with a Gardner 5LW oil engine in 1938, rebodied by Eastern Coach Works in 1949 and withdrawn in 1956. Even at 23 years of age it was thought a useful purchase by the independent Aston, of Marton, Warwickshire.

Below: Postwar Leyland Titan PD2/1 **TD974 (JEL498)** was one a batch of six Leyland-bodied highbridge 56-seat machines, TD972-7, new in 1949, which were later renumbered 1219-24. All six were withdrawn in 1962 and sold for scrap in January 1964. These are both Southampton photographs.

SOUTHDOWN

Above: Dennis Falcon No. **83** (**JUF83**) entered service with Southdown in 1949. It was one of a batch of ten (Nos 82-91) built for the Hayling Island service. Number 83 was withdrawn in 1959. In this 1955 picture it was on excursion work at Portsmouth.

Below: Leyland Cub SKPZ2 No. **7** (**DUF7**) was one of three with Park Royal 26-seat bodies which were new in 1957 for the Hayling Island service. They spent their working lives in the Havant area. The Cub was also on excursion work at Portsmouth in 1955. It was withdrawn in 1956 and became a mobile shop at Kirkby, Lancashire.

PORTSMOUTH

Above: Leyland Titan **152** (**RV9406**) in Portsmouth. This TD4 model dating from 1937 had Cravens 50-seat highbridge bodywork, which was rebuilt by Portsmouth Corporation in 1952. This work extended the vehicle's working life into 1959: having completed 22 years of continuous service, it was sold for scrap in May 1959.

Below: Portsmouth Corporation trolleybus No. **275** (**RV9126**) was an AEC 661T with Cravens 52-seat bodywork, new in November 1936. It was rebuilt, using Metal Sections components, in 1949 by Portsmouth and was withdrawn and scrapped in 1957.

WILTS & DORSET -- Above: Leyland Titan TD1 No. **252 (UF7423)**, seen at Salisbury on 9th August 1954, was one of many TD1s bought by Wilts & Dorset at the start of the Second World War to cope with the troops marshalled in the Salisbury area. It had been new as Southdown No. 923 in 1931 with a Short Bros body and a petrol engine. It was fitted with a Gardner 5LW diesel and Cov-Rad radiator and rebodied by Duple as a 55-seater - all in 1942. The body was rebuilt by Wilts & Dorset in November 1948. Number 252 was sold to a showman in May 1955. *Below:* Leyland Titan TD2 No. **110 (WV2380)**, also at Salisbury on 9th August 1954, had been new to the Company as a Leyland-bodied lowbridge 48-seater in January 1933. Its Leyland petrol engine was exchanged for a Leyland diesel in 1938; a Gardner 5LW was fitted later that year. The Willowbrook body shown was fitted in 1946. The bus was sold, again to a showman, in September 1954.

WILTS & DORSET

Above: Prewar Bristol L5G **504** (**BOW169**) at Salisbury in the rain on 9th August 1954. The Beadle body had been a front-entrance 34-seater. It was rebuilt by the vehicle's first owner, Hants & Dorset, in whose fleet it had been No. 736, as a rear-entrance 32-seater in May 1950. Wilts & Dorset bought the bus in February 1952

Below: This pair of Bristol LS6G saloons, Nos **551** (**JWV762**) and **518** (**HWV946**), dating from 1953 and 1952, had 39 high-backed seats, two doors and an unusual application of the standard Tilling red and cream livery. They were photographed on excursion duties at Bournemouth on 11th August 1954. The dual-door layout was found unsuitable for excursion work and these vehicles were rebuilt as single-door 41-seaters in 1955.

DEVON GENERAL

Above: The Park Royal body on Birmingham's RTs *(see page 43)* bore no visual resemblance to Park Royal bodies on London Transport's contemporary RT chassis; similarly, Weymann bodywork on Devon General's DR326-333 looked unlike the Addlestone factory's work on London vehicles. Number **DR327 (HTT327)**, delivered in 1947, was withdrawn with the rest of the batch in 1960. It later worked for a building contractor.

Below: In its turn, the Weymann body on No. **DR726 (PDV726)** of 1954 looked nothing like that on DR327. It was to the lightweight "Orion" 8ft-wide design with unequal-height windows. Compare its angular, slab-like appearance with that of Hull's No. 338 *(page 42)*, which had the same style of bonnet front-panelling.

SOUTHERN VECTIS

The photographer was fortunate to possess a set of grandparents who lived on the Isle of Wight. As a happy consequence, during a number of summer holidays, the Southern Vectis fleet of the mid 1950s was covered in some detail. Although a Tilling company, there was at that time less standardisation than in many such fleets and some unusual vehicles still earned their keep.

Dennis Aces Nos **400** (**DL9010**), taken on 13th August 1954 at St James Square, Newport; **404** (**DL9014**) in 1955 and **407** (**ADL509**) at Ventnor in 1955 are shown on this page. Bodywork with 20 seats was by Thomas Harrington, of Hove. By the time of these pictures, all three had been fitted with Bedford gearboxes and 6-cylinder petrol engines. They were withdrawn in 1955, 1954 and 1958 to become, respectively, a mobile shop, a garden shed and Boy Scouts' transport. ADL509 was damaged by fire later in 1958 and scrapped.

SOUTHERN VECTIS

Above: Harrington-bodied 35-seat Bristol L5G No. **820** (**CDL611**), photographed by the seaside in 1955. It was fitted when new with a luggage rack, subsequently removed. After withdrawal, only weeks after this picture was taken, No. 820 was sold to a fairground showman.

Below: A happy link between the photographer's home and his summer holidays on the Isle of Wight was provided by ex-SVOC Bristol L5G **BDL853**, running for Durham independent Scarlet Band as fleet number **32**. It was photographed at Seaton Carew in 1955. Originally SVOC No. 805, its bodywork was by John C Beadle, of Dartford. With companion No. 806, it went to Scarlet Band in December 1954.

SOUTHERN VECTIS -- Above: Beadle-bodied, Gardner-engined Leyland Titan TD1 No. **712** (**TK1854**) at Newport on 13th August 1954. This bus was new in 1929 as Hants & Dorset No. E66, fitted with a Beadle highbridge 48-seat open-staircase body. Withdrawn in July 1941 by Hants & Dorset, it turned up with a new Beadle lowbridge body and a Gardner 5LW engine in the Southern Vectis fleet in August 1946. It was withdrawn later in 1954 and ran for Autodrome, of Audenshaw, in the Manchester area, until sold for scrap as a 33-year-old in 1962. *Below:* 1942 Strachans-bodied 55-seat lowbridge Guy Arab No. **900** (**BRD754**), seen at Newport on 18th August 1954, was taken over by SVOC with the business of Enterprise Bus Service, Newport, in June 1951. Enterprise had acquired the Guy from Reading Corporation (Reading's fleet number 6) in March 1950. The vehicle was sold to Bleanch, of Hetton-le-Hole, in 1956, with whom it ran until 1960. It thus completed 18 years in service with its original Ministry of Supply utility specification body.

SOUTHERN VECTIS

Above: Number **703** (**DDL50**), a 1940 Bristol K5G with 56-seat highbridge Eastern Coach Works body, represents the Bristol/ECW combination in the old order. This bus was converted as an open-topper in 1959 and repainted cream. It was used as a tree lopper from 1969 and was sold for preservation in 1979.

Below: The new order by the mid 1950s was the Lodekka, still from Bristol and still with ECW bodywork. Southern Vectis No. **523** (**LDL722**), a 1955 LD6G, was brand new when photographed on service 12 on its way to Freshwater Bay. A 1954 LD6G, No. **509** (**KDL405**), is overtaking on its service 8 run to Shanklin. This photograph is a useful illustration of the first and second styles of grille fitted to early Lodekkas.

SOUTHERN VECTIS

Above: Bedfords **32 (DDL532)** and **30 (ADL392)** at Ryde depot on 15th August 1954. DDL532 was another of the ex-Enterprise vehicles acquired in June 1951. It was an OWB with Duple 26-seat utility bodywork. ADL392 was a 20-seat Duple-bodied WTB model, which had been new to F A Colson, of Carisbrooke, a business taken over by Southern Vectis in March 1939. Again the photographer was just in time, for both were withdrawn in October 1954. *Below:* Duple-bodied 1939 Bedford WTB **CDL729** at Ventnor station in 1955 in the fleet of Nash, of Ventnor, to whom Southern Vectis had sold it in June of that year. It had been SVOC No. 23 and then 207. Nash did not keep the vehicle long: it was noted with Finsbury Coaches, London NW5, in 1956, but was withdrawn by them in April 1957.

SOUTHERN VECTIS

Above: Brand new Bedford SBO No. **226** (**LDL628**), delivered in April 1955 and photographed shortly after, had a Duple 38-seat body. Withdrawn in 1964, after only nine years, it passed to an independent before ending up with Phillips, of Shiptonthorpe, near York, in February 1971. Phillips allegedly withdrew the machine the following month and kept it until December 1986 before disposing of it for scrap. This operator was prone to this kind of thing and had the most amazing collection of derelict vehicles in a large field at Shiptonthorpe.

Below: A pleasant scene at Ventnor in 1955. Lowbridge Bristol K5G No. **705** (**DDL759**) basks in the summer sun alongside Dennis Ace No. **407** (**ADL509**). DDL759 had been new in 1945 as a K6A with a Park Royal highbridge utility 56-seat body and the prewar style of high-mounted Bristol radiator. It was fitted with a 5LW engine and a PV2 radiator, and was rebodied by ECW, in 1953, lasting thus until withdrawal in 1967.

ISLE OF WIGHT INDEPENDENTS 1 -- SHOTTERS

Above: Shotters, of Brighstone, had two of these Daimler CVD6s, registered FDL63/4, with Willowbrook 35-seat bus bodies, bought new in 1947. This one, **FDL63**, was sold in 1956 to Ruby Coaches, of Heather, Leicestershire. The photograph was taken in Newport in 1955.

Below: Shotters bought this attractive fully fronted Seddon IV, **GDL158**, in July 1949. The stylish coachwork was by James Whitson and had 31 seats which were described as "dual-purpose". This is another 1955, nostalgic, warmly sunlit Newport view.

ISLE OF WIGHT INDEPENDENTS 2 -- SEAVIEW SERVICES

Above: Seaview Services Ltd, of Seaview, bought this ex-Rochdale (Rochdale fleet number 135) AEC Regent, **CDK209**, in May 1954 from Boughtons, of London E2, who had acquired it following its withdrawal from the Rochdale fleet in 1953. The body was a 57-seater by Cravens. Seaview ran the bus until November 1959.

Below: Leyland-bodied Titan PD2/1 **GDL764** was bought new by Seaview in May 1950. The lowbridge 53-seat bodywork was painted in a most attractive livery of red and two shades of green. GDL764 has been preserved, but readers not having seen it "in the flesh" can obtain an excellent idea of the livery from the superb 1/76th-scale model of it released in late 2000 by Exclusive First Editions. Both photographs date from 1955.

DENNIS DERELICTION

These former units of the Southern Vectis fleet were found in Jolliffe's scrapyard at Somerton, near Cowes airport, in the summer of 1955. *Above:* Number **12** (**ADL401**) was a 1936 Dennis Lancet 6 with 32-seat coachwork by Harrington, which had been new to Eames, of Shanklin, passing to Southern Vectis in July 1937. It was withdrawn in 1952. *Below:* Number **16** (**ADL400**) had been new in May 1936 to the Isle of Wight Tourist Company, of Ryde, and was a Dennis Lancet with 30-seat coach body by Margham. It was added to the Southern Vectis fleet in June 1938 and withdrawn in 1952. In this view it still has the legend "Cowes Fireworks" in the destination screen.

Number **11** (**DL9719**) was
another ex-Eames Lancet 6,
which had been new in June
1935 with a Duple 32-seat
coach body. It was
withdrawn in 1952 and went
to Jolliffe's yard in January
1953.

Number **6** (**DL7515**), a once-
splendid Dennis Arrow of
June 1931, had a London
Lorries 28-seat coach body
and was another of the
Eames vehicles which SVOC
acquired in July 1937. It was
withdrawn in 1949 and there
is no record of it between
then and its arrival at
Jolliffe's circa 1954.

Dennis Lancet No. **519**
(**DL9709**), bodied as a 36-
seater by Harrington, was
new to Southern Vectis in
July 1935. There is a minor
mystery about this vehicle: it
was withdrawn in 1950, but
its condition in this 1955
view would seem to preclude
it having stood in the open
for five years; equally, its
original, largely undamaged
condition, Southern Vectis
livery (albeit with painted-
out fleetname) and blinds,
perhaps rule out passenger
use with a second owner in
that period.

SEASIDE OPEN-TOP BUSES

Above: This Portsmouth Corporation English Electric-bodied Leyland Titan TD4 of 1935 was No. **115** (**RV6358**). It is seen in this picture at Southsea in 1955. The open-top conversion took place in July 1953. This vehicle is now preserved. *Below:* Gosport & Fareham 1942 K5G Bristol No. **54** (**ECG622**), converted in 1952 and withdrawn in 1969. This is another 1955 photograph.

Opposite page: Hants & Dorset-rebodied (in 1953) 1938 Bristol K5G **1020** (**BTR310**) at Bournemouth on 11th August 1954 *(upper)*; Llandudno & Colwyn Bay Electric Railway Limited Nos **1** and **2** (**HTN231** and **HTN233**) *(centre)*, were ex-Newcastle Corporation (fleet numbers 231/3) 1939 Daimler COG5s with Northern Coachbuilders bodies. Newcastle rebuilt them as open-toppers in May 1952 and they were acquired by Llandudno in April 1956; in the lower picture **HTN233** is seen on 26th June 1954, running as Newcastle Corporation No. **233**.

FROM THE BEST OF THE REST -- Among the many pictures in the David Burnicle collection which remained after the categories illustrated in the preceding pages had been chosen, these two cried out for inclusion at, it must be stated, the expense of many another of equal interest. Creamline's half-decker "Irene" (**KHO178**) was in Newcastle *(above)* on 1st August 1953. The chassis was a Crossley SD42/9 and the 48-seat coachwork was by Mann Egerton to a Lincs Trailer Company design. **GF7254** *(below)* was built by the LGOC at Chiswick in 1930 as one of four experimental 54-seat double-deckers fitted with Meadows petrol engines. As bonnet-number LT1000, it was withdrawn by the LPTB in May 1939 and sold to a dealer. The body, shown here, later carried by GF7254 was by Duple, and was originally fitted to a Tilling-Stevens "Successor" six-wheeled coach chassis exhibited at the 1937 Earls Court Show. The Tilling-Stevens may never have run under its own power, but its body resurfaced after the war on GF7254 in the fleet of White Heather Transport Limited, of Southsea. The Tilling-Stevens had been underfloor-engined (with eight cylinders, at that), with a set-back front axle; thus much remodelling was necessary to fit the body to a front-engined ex-London Transport bus chassis with a longer wheelbase. This remarkable vehicle was converted as a caravan after White Heather had finished with it and it eventually went for scrap in 1961. Of all the missed preservation projects over which we agonise, this would have been one of the most unusual and valuable, combining as it did some exotic prewar experimental work from both London General at Chiswick and Duple Motor Bodies at Hendon. *(The writer is grateful to Alan Townsin, who explained the fascinating story of GF7254's later history in his book "Duple: 70 Years of Coachbuilding", published by Venture Publications Ltd in 1998.)*